THE TRANSCENDENCE

MARA RECALIS

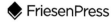 FriesenPress

One Printers Way
Altona, MB R0G 0B0
Canada

www.friesenpress.com

ISBN
978-1-03-913381-5 (Hardcover)
978-1-03-913380-8 (Paperback)
978-1-03-913382-2 (eBook)

1. SELF-HELP, SPIRITUAL

Distributed to the trade by The Ingram Book Company

For my Beloved sister,
Nina

I wish you all the joy that you can wish

The Merchant of Venice, William Shakespeare
(3.2.194)

Some Things Never Change

It is nineteen ninety-seven and as I sit, milking the cow, I cannot help but wonder how on earth I am breaking a sweat, and what the path was that led me here in the first place. I can feel my back quivering with salted exuberance in a buffet of humus, as if I were deeply grounded in Gaia herself. My deeply-pocketed hands ache now, and I am done for the day.

Good Old Nellie, as I am so fond of calling her, slowly turns from me and profiles her surroundings. Then, she is gone. As she abandons me, alone in my wonderfully miserable trembling of insecurity and questioning, I begin to shake. And, I cannot stop.

"My name is Holland, Holland Millar! Do you hear me? I SAID, MY NAME IS HOLLAND MILLAR!" No response. I can't believe this bellowing is soaring out of my mouth. And who am I crying out for help to? As I look around, I see no one. There is a desolate vacuum here, a vastness to my transparency. I am alone, and yet I feel more connected and in my body than ever before. Maggie was right – nature and animals certainly have a powerful and cathartic healing effect on us.

I can barely stand now. This dusty, oxygen-deprived lime green barn smells like baked peach cobbler, on a hazy humid summer afternoon. Wait a minute – that smell again. Why is the room starting to sp…sp…?

As I awake from my glorious unconscious visit to the depths of my being, I begin to survey my surroundings. *My body is shuddering with massive confusion.*

"Maggie, where am I? Was I sleeping?"

"Holly, you are in the hospital. Everything is okay. You just passed out. Sam thought it was best to call an ambulance, to be on the safe side. He said you experienced another healing response. He's here with Carol, and they are out in the hallway. How do you feel?"

"I ache all over. Are you sure this was just a healing response?" I'm scared.

"Yes. It's common for some people to experience it like this. Remember, you were also very active all day, using muscles you didn't know you had…"

"I do enjoy showing-off for you, my love." I know it may sound cliché but I am so happy when Maggie is with me, and I feel safe with her, especially as I experience this unknown territory. She eternally urges me to persevere, even when nothing is what I think it will be. That is what I continue to learn over and over again – that *nothing is what I think it will be.*

⁑

It is now nineteen ninety-five, and here I am standing in the hallway of our humble abode, silently observing my wife read the letter that saves our marriage:

My Beloved Margaret,

You were right. I am a cynical, institutionalized slab of grey cement in urban academia. I am a miserable, old sod.
I write to you now, and promise, I will not use my big fancy words when I speak to you. You are a very intelligent and enlightened woman, and yes, I am pretentious. This has been my conditioning. It is time for me to see through your eyes, feel through your heart, and know through your soul. Anything is possible. I meditate now, and I understand.
Forgive me, and please be patient with me. I need your guidance and support now.

Your loving husband forever,
Holland

Tears stream down her face as she giggles, and quietly reads my letter to herself. Her dove-like right palm rests on her ample bosom, and she lets out a slow breath through her rounded, cherry-red lips. She is beaming, and she suddenly looks like she is twenty years younger, sitting in front of our hearty, rustic-hued fireplace.

Maggie stands up from her ascot-patterned recliner, and confidently sways towards me now; her full body oscillating with each step. She gently places her arms around my sinewy neck, and then exhales, deeply.

"Welcome home, Holly. Welcome home."

⟿

As I lie here in bed, alone in my antiseptic-smelling hospital room, I notice red, green, and yellow rainbows painted on all four of the walls. I cannot believe it has been two years to the day that Maggie read the letter. I will never forget what happened on that humid afternoon when I wrote it. The sky was a hazy powder blue, and there was a faint stillness in the air. My radiant-looking five year old granddaughter was visiting with us, along with our spirited and extremely talented daughter, Emma. Alice was angelically chanting something in the next room, as her mother was drumming:

Boom, hmmm, Boom, hmmm, ahma, ohma, ahma, ohma,
Boom, hmmm, Boom, hmmm, ahma, ohma, ahma, ohma,
Boom, hmmm, Boom, hmmm, ahma, ohma, ahma, ohma,
Boom, hmmm, Boom, hmmm, ahma, ohma, ahma, ohma…

Maggie was in the kitchen baking peach cobbler, and its cinnamon aroma permeated right through me. I broke down, and with my highly cerebral and heavy head in my deeply-pocketed hands, I began sobbing, silently and intensely. I cannot remember the last time that I cried.

Carol and Sam Beach are teaching me, throughout this sacred transformation, that I am experiencing healing responses which are triggered by childhood memories that make me feel safe and nurtured. …*Mother…*

This was the first time that I accompanied Maggie to one of her group meditations on the Beachs' farm, and it was my saving grace – my buoyant lifeline to the happiness and fulfillment, joy, peace and ease that I have been searching for, in my head, all of my life. Who knew that the answer was as simple as being in the present moment, through deep breathing and connecting with your body. I have finally learned to befriend who I already am. And I can honestly say that I love and accept myself, faults and all. If nature is an imperfect display of perfection, then so am I. I have diligently researched and debated this mystery continually in my academic circle for many a year now, to no conclusion. And I just may have found some answers by going within. I am content in my knowing of these truths.

A Birthday Haiku
Blessings of Joy, Peace and Love –
And, eyes wide twinkling.
Happy Birthday Holls!
All our love, Carol and Sam Beach

My barrel-shaped and generously immense belly is aching. I am now finishing an enormous bout of laughter with this kind birthday card that I received from two of our best friends, and I don't understand why I am reacting to it like this.

I smell vanilla…

"Hey Dad, are you there?" Calls Emma, as she opens our front door, and peeks in.

I don't respond.

"Hey, birthday boy, I have something for you!"

Nothing.

"Dad? You here? Anyone home? C'mon Dad, I know you're here…" She is all the way in the toasty warm hallway now, and her voice echoes sweetly towards me. She knows I'm here. I could never fool her. She is my one and only.

"I'm in the kitchen, Emma. Enter if you dare." I finally answer.

"There you are. I knew I'd find you in here. Happy birthday." She bends over and plants a soft peck on my distinguished, bearded right cheek. I always light up when I see Emma. She looks so much like her mother.

"Thank-you, Emms. Sit with me until your mother gets home. She's at the bakery, picking out my favourite celebratory 'Old Crony' cake." I muse.

"Look at all these birthday cards! You certainly are a popular guy."

"I feel blessed."

Emma smiles gently and bends over again, this time kissing my forehead. She softly squeezes my right hand, and then glides onto the chair next to me, like a beautiful white dove floating down to her ancestral, chocolate-brown nest.

"Joshua is coming by with Alice after work. He wanted to bring our gift to you himself. I think he is still trying to win your approval."

"I'll make him sweat a little longer, the poor chap." I say. I hope they got me the inuksuk I wanted.

"And I thought you mellowed."

Emma and I have always had a very close bond and good rapport. Thank goodness some things never change. She is quite ecstatic about her life now. I am thankful she and Josh survived and thrived through their first real and difficult testing period, in their four year marriage. They made it through. We all did.

The copper kettle starts to whirr, and a thick layer of steam billows above our heads, enveloping the dimly-lit, mustard yellow kitchen we seat ourselves in. The kettle's whistling is an interesting companion to the classical melodies of Tchaikovsky's scene from Act Two in Swan Lake, playing in the background. I cherish these moments alone with my daughter.

"I'll pour us a cup of Earl Grey, Dad."

"Sounds good. So tell me, how was your day? Any new epiphanies?" Her gentle strength and wise compassion astound me.

She has risen above me. The student is teaching the teacher now, and I sit patiently, listening intently, as I give her all of my attention. Her carousel of fragrant honeydew and mint light flows in every direction. And she is glowing. There is a prism of right-rounded, glimmering-gold vitality that she radiates towards me, and I am open to receiving this energy exchange. I have taught her well, and realize that she is my legacy.

"Yes. I have understood that I have so many layers to me – so much more to discover and explore. Joshua loves it, and little Ally keeps seeing so much more of me than I have ever seen. Children are incredible that way. They can see and mirror the wonder of life in us through their clear and honest lens of non-judgment and unconditionality. That is how she is teaching me. I see myself through her gorgeous orbs of wisdom. She is definitely an old soul."

I am smiling in awe, and nodding with validation. I remember when Emma began teaching me those lessons.

"What is it, Dad? Why are you looking at me that way?"

"It's nothing, Emma. Please, continue."

The Sestina
On The Mountaintop

We awoke in the East, with a glorious rising sun,
And we now bear witness to the Super New Moon.
It is such an honour
To be sweetly satiated with our Creator's Compassion,
And our source of Divine Justice –
As we experience our Right Rounded Chi of completion.

What life situation of yours is ready for completion?
It radiates an impassioned flame in you that blazes like the sun.
It is time now to pray for some Universal Justice –
An outstretched hand from above, pulling on your Tui of emotion, like the moon.
My spontaneous attitude of loving-kindness, and compassion
Enlivens your forest-green Garden of Honour.

It is a protective tablecloth of Truth that you must honour,
A boomerang of Karma in Completion –
And an ancient, mystical exuberance of compassion.
Like the Splendour of Sun,
And the Goddess Intuition of Moon –
Here, now, the pewter scales of balanced justice.

The Transcendence

My wisdom strengthens us in our journey towards justice –
And we will right all wrongs, for honour.
A morality in her Waxing Moon
Furnishes a fruitful bowl of Completion.
My rays of luxurious Light are of the sun,
Guiding you with spiraling Orbs of compassion.

Our choice to act with compassion
Invokes triumphant and jubilant Archangels of justice,
Warming our hearts with the prisms of the sun
That we must continue to Honour.
Our carousel of courage and completion –
To be, just as we are, here and now in the moment of the moon.

Meditating on the Mountaintop of Moon
We are gently caressed by compassion –
In the rings of Saturn with Ascension of Masters, there is completion.
Our cosmic cycles of justice
Bestow unto us a worthiness in its Highest Honour –
That brightens our soul with the vitality of the sun.

This new moon activates the values of compassion and completion, shining like the sun.
You act with compassion in the completion stage of cultivating your honour.
I am supported with compassion, in the completion stage of my quest for divine justice.

Keeping The Faith

This small town looks rustic. The population here is one-thousand, seven-hundred and fifty. The bird's-eye view of this magical place, as we are landing in the mighty Seven Forty Seven, is one of a microcosm within a great macrocosm; a bustling community amongst nature's grandeur. All of these majestic red rocks that surround it nestle this safe haven, for those of us who are looking – and for those of us who are seeking. Carol and I are two of those people.

As my love of many years and I hike deeper and deeper within the winding trail of the canyon, I mistakenly bump into her, as she pauses to look at a Two-Tailed Swallowtail butterfly on the dusty-rose ground to our right.

"Sam, look at this. Isn't it beautiful? I wonder if it's a male or a female."

"It's a female. I can tell by the orange tint in its body. Quite a beaut."

"She sure is."

As I glance at Carol's face, she reminds me of an awestruck teenager, viewing a masterpiece on canvas for the very first time. Her bone-straight shiny black hair flows down to the small of her back…her deep blue penetrating eyes…and her earthy brown eyelashes. *I realize that she is the masterpiece, and I am the awestruck teenager, at her mercy. Carol is gorgeous.*

The time is now eleven thirty-one in the morning, and my stomach is growling like a ferocious father bear protecting his cubs. It feels like a dull, grueling ache. And as I look up, the landscape begins to spin.

"Baby, where's the breakfast?" I ask.

"You ate it in the restaurant. Are you still hungry?"

"You know me, Mister Wooden-leg."

"Well, Mister Wooden-leg, here is a peanut-butter and banana sandwich, made especially for you growing boys." And thankfully, she hands me the food.

"Why are you so good to me? You know I love you." I am keeping it light.

"Of course."

Man, do I ever need to sit down and eat. Now. "Let's stop and rest awhile."

"Sounds good."

Just as Carol says those words, I find a large bronze-coloured rock that is shaped like a mushroom. The rock even smells mouldy and sweet, yet it is making for a splendid makeshift picnic table, and I am famished. I start to eat slowly, only biting tiny amounts of this fresh creamy meal, and I am chewing each morsel thoroughly, savouring its soft velvet texture and salty-sweet, nutty flavour, in my salivating mouth. I cannot help but gaze admiringly at Carol. But she is somewhere else in her thoughts.

"Do you remember when we first met?" She asks me suddenly, and with some trepidation in her voice. She is looking at the stunning diamond ring on her finger, that I gave her two years earlier.

"What's going on?"

"Well, do you?"

"Yeah, of course. The night I met you was the night I knew that I wanted to marry you. I knew you were the right one for me then, and I know it now. You know that." Here it comes…

"Yes…Sam, I'm sorry that I've kept you waiting, with this beautiful engagement ring on my finger. I know I keep using the excuse of waiting for both of our kids to move out of the house before we get married, but…I'm scared." A tear is rolling down the left side of her face.

"What is it that you're afraid of?" I pull her to me, and hold her in my arms.

"Well, I know you're nothing like he was, and I'm happy with you."

"Are you sure?"

"Am I sure, what…?"

"That you're happy with me." She is pausing. I feel like someone just kicked me in the gut.

"Yes, I am happy with you." Suddenly, I lose my robust appetite, and I gently lay my sandwich down on the mushroom rock.

"Carol, be honest with me. Are you truly happy with me? Do you still love me?" She starts to kiss me all over my face, smiling at me as she runs her delicate fingers through my thinning hair.

"I love you. I was hoping that this trip would revive something in us – a rekindling of sorts. But now I realize that we really need to go back to couples counseling, as soon as we get home. I have to understand why I can't get past what he did, and why I am so unhappy within myself. Sam, will you continue to support me, and wait for me?"

"Yeah. Even though digging deeper with my emotions is hard for me, I'm always here for you, and I always will be." In all of my forty-eight years, I have never loved someone the way that I love her. *Going to couples counseling works for us.*

Deep within the amber hues of the canyon, the brilliant citrine rays of the sun shine through the emerald-green line of trees that surround us, and I look up in gratitude. The temperature suddenly rises, and we remove our jackets as we pack our belongings, and get ready to drag ourselves back to our hotel room. A dry, warm wind from the west circles behind us.

The Sonnet
Right Rounded Chi

Upon induction into such a fray

Left tendency guiding your way,

Always rushing, forcing and fouling

Then you entertain us with your howling.

Chaos and confusion, decimation attempted

Your maneuvering holds no power, and we are exempted.

Bitterness emanates from you, negativity is your muse

Your stairway is betrayal and we have nothing to lose.

We allow your zig-zag to become a straight line –

It is now that our Love and Light begins to shine,

And we act with turns of Right Rounded Chi

Inspiring three opposite doorways; replenishing cups of Chai.

Our popularity, like sunny windows of balance,

Our Divinity of Deity like rainbows of freelance.

When Angels Call

"How To Know God" by Deepak Chopra. "Creative Visualization" by Shakti Gawain. "Heal Your Body A-Z" by Louise L. Hay. "The Art of Happiness" by His Holiness the Dalai Lama. I am impressed. Dr. Pfeiffer has quite the collection of healing tools and resources here, resting like a shiny gold decorative fan, on her iron and glass waiting room table of self-discovery and spiritual healing.

Suddenly, my hazel eyes fixate themselves upon the book *"How To Know God"*. I feel mesmerized by it.

"Constance, she's ready for you now" chirps her secretary, Betty. This woman frustrates me – she continually calls me by my birth name, after I have repeatedly asked her not to. She must be old school.

I feel compelled to bring that mesmerizing book in with me, as I enter her counseling room. But once again, I resist. That's me – either I sit on the fence, or I resist.

"Hey Connie, come on in and have a seat. Make yourself comfortable." The good doctor greets me with a warm smile today.

"Thanks, Dr. Pfeiffer. Don't mind if I do." I sit myself down on her forest-green, chenille-pillowed couch. I'm sinking deeply into them now; pillows cascading around both sides of my body, there to nurture and protect me for my journey within. I feel fortunate that I was able to get this short appointment with her today, based on the fact that it is the Christmas holidays, and she was able to fit me in.

"Okay, Connie. Tell me, how are you feeling today?"

"I feel tired. I'm still processing quite a bit from our last session, and I am expressing it in my journal, like you suggested. I'm journaling all the time now. And when I write it down, I experience my epiphanies."

"Does writing it down help you to make sense of your experiences, and understand yourself better?" She asks me, cautiously.

"Yes. When I combine this work with the deep-breathing exercises that you gave me, I often feel tension in various parts of my body. What does that mean?" I question Dr. Pfeiffer, hoping that she has the answer for me.

"It means that you are healing. A person cannot heal unless they do some form of therapeutic bodywork on themselves, because everything we experience, we store on a cellular level within our bodies. And, everything that we experience in our relationships, with ourselves and others, are energy exchanges and dynamics. It's all based in quantum physics. Science supports it, and it tends to be a fascinating read. Does this make sense to you?"

"I sort of understand what you are saying. It helps to explain behaviours. Once I began to see my parents' marriage dynamics from that perspective, control issues and all, I became more at peace with their divorce. I was young at the time, and divorce was frowned upon in my familial background. All I was doing was coping and surviving. All of the work we've done has helped me to heal from and release the conditioning and patterns that ended up leading to my divorce. I was just repeating what my mother did…" I could go on and on about this.

As I peek over and look just beyond Dr. Pfeiffer, I see a crystal clock, hanging high above on her dusty-rose coloured wall. She has finally hung her medical degree from university to the right of it, situated directly behind her blue-green, stony-topped, iron-legged desk. *Feng shui*. It's good to see it there, in full view. She should be very proud of it – she definitely earned it. I know that Dr. Pfeiffer wasn't always there for her daughter Alice, in her younger years. The med-school workload. It was her full-time job, and she was married to it for many years. But, that is another chapter…

"Good for you. I am proud to have such a committed young woman as my patient. You have made progress by leaps and bounds."

"Thanks to you…"

"Connie, you are the one doing the work. I am just here to facilitate and support you in your journey. And now, I would like to make one more suggestion, if you're open to receiving this help." She is smiling again. She looks radiant, and that is causing me to feel angry. I tend to react this way when I am in the company of beauty. However, I trust her – she continues to pass the tests that I give her. Dr. Pfeiffer seems to know exactly what it is that I need, and what I am ready for.

"Okay. I'm open, and I trust you."

"In order to heal, there has to be forgiveness: of the self and from others. And we must also forgive. So, how about starting a personal ritual every morning, of prayer?" She is really feeling me out here.

"Prayer? Me pray? I haven't done that in years – not since my parents' divorce." Suddenly, I feel uncomfortable, and at the same time, very much in need of this. My path, until I was referred to Dr. Pfeiffer, never seemed to be the right one for me. I had turned my back on God, and I have been consumed by jealousy, negativity and bitterness. I have overheard others describe me as being a critical, manipulative, two-faced mean girl – like a viper, a wasp. It's no wonder I have not been well-liked. I *believed* that I was, but…

"So, Connie, are you willing to ask the Divine for help? And let it light the way for you again?" She asks me, with optimism.

"Um, let me think about it." My guard is up again, and I am breaking out in a cold sweat.

"Okay, sounds good."

As my therapy session ends, Dr. Pfeiffer escorts me into the airy and brightly-lit waiting room. That's when she hands me the healing modality pamphlets I asked for: Certified Reflexology, Network Spinal Analysis, Usui-Do, and Registered Holistic Nutrition. I happen to look outside, and notice that the snowfall is quite heavy. I'm not worried because I live only a few blocks away, and the walk home will do me some good; all that fresh air and exercise.

As I step out into the spiraling white flurry of nature's dance, my legs begin to quiver, and I rapidly sink into the huge snowdrift that glitters with gold speckles of ivory diamonds. I feel like I am a kid again, shuffling and wading through this cold, billowy mass of winter – hungry, and hurrying home to the safety of…of what? I never felt safe at home. This sudden realization scares me. I never felt safe at home – so much hate. Maybe I should walk through the park and…*I never felt safe, as a child, in my home.*

If I don't get home right away, they will come looking for me. Here is the merry-go round. I'll just sit here and wait. Mom and Dad will find me, so worried that they have lost me, and they will promise to never ever be mean again. Yeah, this will work.

As I sit down, I can feel the deep freeze permeate my entire body. I begin to shake, and I cannot stop yawning. It's really cold out here – the temperature must have rapidly dropped in the last few minutes.

It's getting dark too, and the snowfall is as thick as a great Peruvian waterfall – a cascading movement of delicate snowflakes that intoxicate me. Wait, what time is it?

Gusts of wind howl around me, like a ravenous pack of coyotes sensing that their prey is near. This blowing ferocity numbs me, on every level of my being. As I put my left hand in front of my face, it disappears into what looks to be a vacuum of white butterflies, fluttering around and around. I hear a high-pitched melody; a swooning serenade of stillness that softens and warms my heart. It fills me with a joyous love and deep sense of peace that I have not known before. Now, I am completely saturated by a giggling array of light-green and pink bubbles that illuminate a path in front of me. I become aware that I have been praying and crying this whole time, and I didn't even know it.

Something compels me to stand up and follow this heavenly champagne of bouncing spheres that adorn me. As I do, I begin to cross-country ski through this thigh-high frozen moisture, knowing that I must continue to move forward. And...*trust.*

ево

Subject: Thank-you

Dear Dr. Pfeiffer,

It has been one year since that fateful day, and I still have no recollection of how I
made it home from your office. I just knew that something greater than me was in charge,
saving my life and changing me for the better. I got a second chance at life,
and it's a good one. I have connected with God, and it is on a level that I didn't know was possible. I was not able to talk about my spiritual experience, my rebirth, so here
it is in a poem that I wrote for you. I hope it gives you the solace, guidance,
and inspiration that you have so generously given to me.

"Untitled"

If you call to me, I will answer
Forgiveness as your gift
As I make my right turn in my time of need,
And face you again.

You have answered my prayer,
And you continue to love me, without conditions.

I will follow your ways from now on –
As we are within each other
And I am blessed.

A luminous light of Angels
Surround me now, forever.

Again, you have birthed me –
You have saved me from myself.
I will never abandon you again.

A fulfillment in life now,
So grandiose and sacred.
I had no happiness before you.

What was it to live, to love? Where was my goodness?
I was filled with such lies, hypocrisies and facades.
And, I was consumed in a buzz of jealousy
As I plead my immoral alliance
To those who were of a negative influence –
Supporting my scornfully bitter character.

My amendment to all continues
As you strengthen, heal, and guide me.
I redeem myself to those who will forgive me.
And I accept all consequences –
For now I am truly free.

The Sonnet
Right Rounded Transcendence

You approach us with such jealousy, in you there is ire
Your underworld of anguish; you are lost in your mire.
As we remove your mask, and behold you in sin –
Your sable of sadness, so dark and so dim.
Buzzing near us, always tricking to the left –
Enacting your own defeat, that causes your own cleft.
In you there is wickedness – you are a viper, a wasp
And we release you from our lives now, for your power amounts to a wisp.
We allow your zig-zag to become a straight line –
It is now that our Love and Light begins to shine,
And we act with turns of Right Rounded Transcendence
Inspiring many lifetimes for your repentance.
Our popularity, like sunny windows of balance,
Our Divinity of Deity like rainbows of freelance.

Seasons For Understanding

Really, I am not looking forward to dissecting this cadaver. After all, it is Joshua's birthday today – and besides, who wants to be thinking, no, immersing yourself in death when *there is so much about life to celebrate*. Yet here I am, digging in. It has a fibrous, tough, and dense feel to it. There is cirrhosis here – and it seems to weigh more than it should. Thud. Yes, I was right – it's massive. How could someone do this to their own body, their sacred temple? If only he could have felt what I do, he may have taken better care of…

"Emma, are you here? Earth calling Emma – come in Emma." Adele jokes.

"Oh, sorry Adele. I must've been fully focused again. What is it?" I reply, with sincerity.

"Class is over. Let's take a break before we have to begin our *time* in Emerg. It is beautiful outside; let's de-stress in nature."

"Right. Good idea. I'm glad that a part of our schooling is in a hospital that is nicely nestled in the valley. And, thank God we won't be *on call one in two* for our future internship, like they used to do. It was such a dangerous protocol. I don't think I will be able to be fully alert and functional for my up and coming rounds, based on my current workload. I can only imagine how it will be four years from now."

"I agree. Hopefully this break will bring in some much needed sanity too." Adele emphasizes this point.

"You've got that right." How true. Thankfully, she is here to ground me. Adele nurtures me like a mother hen. And I'm glad she has decided to specialize in pediatrics.

As I look outside, I feel strongly compelled to focus on the crested and colourful treeline just to the north of us. "Let's get out of here. Now."

I am pulled into a vortex of crimson – a plentiful plethora of reds, yellows, and coppers. *The fall colours.* As I breathe in a dense and earthy humus, I feel delighted to be alive. My energy is soaring, and I feel at one with *All That Is.* Thank you Mother Earth, for your generous and life-sustaining harvest of gifts. The healer is the one that is being healed.

"So, how is sweet little Alice? Did you get a chance to see her before you got here?" Adele asks, cautiously.

"No. Joshua had already brought her to the daycare by the time I got up. And, it's his birthday today – the first one that we won't be spending together since I've been with him." There is a roundness to my tone, and a hollow emptiness in my answer. My eyes begin to swell with such glassy, guilt-ridden tears, and my heart is aching. *Aching to be with my beloveds.* Alice is too young to be without her mother. She's only two years old. And Joshua…

"It feels like someone is pressing on my sternum, and that my ribcage is imploding." I sputter, as I begin to gasp for air.

"Calm down, Emma. *Breathe, slowly.* Yes, that's it. Good. Everything will be okay, just focus and breathe in…and breathe out. That's it, right. You got it. *Slowly breathe in, and release. Good…good.*"

As I begin to breathe more steadily, I realize that I was also sobbing, deeply. I feel as if I just died. My nose feels swollen and is plugged, and there is a metallic taste in my mouth. *Adele is apologizing to me – profusely.* It's okay though; it was only a matter of time before I really allowed myself to *go there.* And I certainly did. It is a good process that she facilitated for me, and I am thankful for that. I was getting a bit concerned because I was starting to feel emotionally detached, and painfully numb: the warning signs of *shutting down.*

I can honestly say that *slash and burn medicine* will definitely not be my thing. To open people up who are in need of critical care? No. It took everything in me to not faint at the sight of my first post-surgical patient, during my interviewing session in hospital this morning. I hope my face didn't reflect what I was thinking, and feeling. It was so hard to see someone with a portion of their face gone – all because they didn't wear their seatbelt. *I have to get this image out of my mind now, and focus on my drive home;* the roads are very slippery, and I want to take my time. Joshua is waiting for me. I hope the dinner he made isn't getting cold, again.

The streetlights are aglow with a fuzzy amber hue, as if they were halos adorning a divine procession of angels, all waiting patiently to receive their wings. Suddenly, I feel warm and comfortable.

It is as if I were wrapped in golden spiritual blankets of unconditional love and understanding; mesmerized by a crackling stream of yellow and orange spiraling fireplace flames. Ah…here's my humble abode. As I pull up, I can see that Joshua has placed our Christmas tree in the front window. It will look beautiful, once we decorate it tonight. I am so excited. We are finally going to have our festive evening together, as a family. I have grown to cherish these occasions.

It doesn't seem like more than a month has already passed since the New Year began, and we are certainly getting a lot of heavy snow. Maybe that brown hawk will perch itself on my backyard oak again, like it did this time last year. To be honest, I cannot believe it is our second wedding anniversary today, and I have it off. I've been away so much since I started medical school, and it has been taking its toll on our marriage. It's been a challenging adjustment so far, and I am so thankful that Joshua is very understanding and supportive of what I do. This is definitely our test.

As I gently float our white tablecloth over our cherry-wood dining room table, its golden embroidered and looped edging catches my eye. I am in amazement of the artisan's creative talent. I wonder where Mom purchased it. It was part of the wedding gift that was given to us from my parents, and I can tell that it is hand-made. As I set the table with our best crystal and china, that were also wedding gifts, I feel the spirit of generosity wash over me, like a mist of light rain, shimmering down from above. Whenever we use these patterns, it is a loving reminder to me of kindness and goodwill. They didn't have to gift us with all of this, considering the fact that we eloped. But I'm happy that they did. Now, my silver-plated flatware, that was handed down to me, completes my canvas – a canvas of the culinary kind. I polished all of it this morning, and they sparkle like the beads of diamonds, resting atop a still and silent winter's lake, while the sun shines its brilliance for all to admire. Herein lies the serenity of design.

Alice is with Mom, so that Joshua and I can finally have some alone time together. I hope that he enjoys my prime rib, with all the trimmings. It smells succulent; the aroma of seasonings magically mystifies the air, and makes me salivate, wanting to dig-in. As I start to pirouette into the kitchen, my husband is standing right in front of me, and he is smiling *that smile*. He holds his hand up, and smoothly gestures to me so that I will dance with him. He pulls me very close, and *I am now completely enveloped in him.* His fingers caress the small of my back, and I move to his circular rhythms. Our stirring is a slow and steady sway, and it is at this very moment that we pledge to never, ever, let each other go.

I love how my garden tulips have sprung up in a vibrant array of purples, pinks and reds. We had a burst of hot weather, and the budding greens and rainbows of primaries have opened in a blossoming of innocent youth. There is a sense of excitement in the air; I feel like my new blooms are messages of increasing love, faith, and unity, and I could really benefit from all three. Especially now.

Tap tap tap, at my front door. I think Mom is finally here. Now we can have that heart-to-heart talk that I have been patiently waiting for. I am starting to feel somewhat down about the pressures of school, and how it is affecting my marriage.

"C'mon in, Mom. The door is open." I think she heard me.

"Emma, dear, where are you?"

"I'm in the solarium." I am the most comfortable in this room.

"Ah, I found you. I knew you'd be in here. It is the first room that I always check." I guess Mom didn't hear me after all.

As I rise to greet her with a warm hug and a loving kiss, I start to feel safe, and happy to be seeing her again. I have really missed her and the talks that continue to bond us. We are very close, and we've always enjoyed our mutually positive, supportive, and respectful mother-daughter relationship.

"I've steeped some chamomile tea for us, Mom. Would you like some?"

"Of course. I'm feeling a bit jumpy from the drive here, and this should settle me down."

Just as I pour the tea in her porcelain, pink, rose-patterned cup – she always drinks from a cup and saucer – Mom sits down right by my side, and smiles that sincere smile of hers. "Emma, what is troubling you? You sounded upset on the phone last night. Tell me dear, what is it?"

My body begins to tremble as I hand Mom her tea. "It's Joshua and I. We're not communicating, and I am concerned. I'm away so much, and he's the one with all the domestic responsibilities. He does the cooking, cleaning, laundry, and is the one taking care of Alice most of the time. He brings her to and picks her up from daycare, feeds and bathes her, reads to her, plays and talks with her. Then Joshua puts her to bed, and gets her ready for the next day to do it all over again. I think he is angry with me. He has no time for himself after he gets home from work, and he's had to make sacrifices – we both have. I even missed his birthday last year, and he wasn't too happy about it."

"Emma, this is a temporary re-adjustment in the big picture of your marriage. I know it must not be easy, but you will all make it through." She pauses for a few seconds to sip her tea. "Think of it this way: women of your generation *love* having a man that can take care of himself, and who can support and care for them in every way. And, my sweet Alice is bonding with her daddy. How many girls growing up get a chance to spend that much time with their fathers?"

Her words are comforting. And it's true – I always wished that I could have spent more time with Dad when I was growing up. "You're right, I know, but it hurts not to be with her too. I'm happy that she is becoming close with Joshua, but I feel so guilty. A little girl needs her mother. *We need each other.*"

"And that will come, more so at the right time. I *know* that *Josh deeply loves you* and is very proud of you. And I don't think he is mad at you. I think he just *misses you.* We all understand that you are doing what you are here to do, and you have our full support. Josh is a very understanding man, and I think he needs some support himself."

"In what way?"

"Let him know that he can call me anytime if he needs help. I can also come over when he is alone and cook dinner, and perhaps do some laundry, if he'd like…"

"Thanks, Mom. That would be great. I will talk to him and let you know. I really appreciate that you would do this. I love you."

"I love you too."

↬

It's nice to just be lying here listening to the meditative and melodic chants of the crickets. The humidity this evening is sky-high; it is like a thick, soupy mass of heavy rain that hovers and surrounds you, keeping you very still. My sweet girl is asleep beside me now, with her fairy-goddess doll cradled in her arms. *They make a good pair.* Of course, I read *"Green Eggs and Ham" by Dr. Seuss* to Alice three times before she allowed her magical dream world to whisk her away, and enchant her with a wonder that only a child co-creates.

I wonder what adventure is calling to her tonight, and what path her fairies are leading her on. Are you flying high above the clouds with your angel wings carrying you? Are you in a magical garden, where all of your dreams have come true? Are you playing with the angels, or are you swimming with the dolphins? Only my little one knows.

"Alice, tell Mommy what your dreams are, and I will make them come true for you. I promise. I love you baby – I always will. I will always be here with you in your dreams." I whisper…

As I look over her and glance at our favourite painting on the wall, my heart and mind are now with Joshua - *my Right One*, my true love. We are so good together. He would do anything for me,

I am confident of that. *We make a good pair.* And, I know that he has always appreciated that I supported him in similar ways, throughout university.

I hope he is having a good time out tonight at the ballgame, with Dad. They have become closer lately, and he really wants to impress Dad. I think Joshua is seeking parental approval. Dad better go easy on him. Wait a minute…since when does Dad like baseball?

The Sestina
Look Upon The Stars

Your hazy gaze now focused on the stars
Mesmerized at their brilliance – their spatial integrity,
And your wellspring of respect
Guides you to your truth.
Roaring with Golden fires of dancing growth; you now have a responsibility –
It is your Acclaim to be kind.

You are marvelous when you paint your masterpiece – when you are kind.
Each Noble stroke of brush is a Divine explosion on your canvas of stars,
And you act with responsibility.
Your followers adore your dazzling cascade of sparkled integrity.
Now, you are in your truth –
Tell me, how do you feel when you treat yourself with respect?

Towards all females, and those older than you – give them your gift of respect;
They have walked in your shoes, and they return it in kind.
From them you will quietly Master rippling tides of truth,
And you admire them – they reside in the Stars.
Beaming down tropical sandcastles, from the Islets of Integrity –
A Summer Solstice of Responsibility.

The Transcendence

Great effortlessness and ease bubbles up, in your Humane responsibility
To treat all life with respect.
When you act with integrity
The World will respond, and be kind.
It is written in the stars;
A cozy cultivation – a rosy ripening of toasty truth.

This mellowing marshmallow that bakes in your Amber fires of truth,
Helps you to come clean, and accept responsibility.
And you pause awhile to look upon the stars,
Reflecting on your artwork of Respect.
You are One of a Kind –
A magnet of Magenta, with scores of integrity.

There is tremendous value and talent in an act of Integrity –
A wealth of cash that nestles my Garnet and Peridot of Truth;
I appreciate you, and I thank you for being kind.
The Right Roundedness to all acts of accepting responsibility
Resonates with a Richness of Respect,
And an Omnipotent co-creation in the Heavenly Stars.

My intentions that contain integrity and truth will glow in kind, like the stars.
My acts of integrity and truth are born from a kind sense of self-respect.
Your acts of integrity and truth are born from a kind sense of self-responsibility.

Coming Full Circle

It is my eighteenth birthday this weekend, and I am finally allowed to journey at the Beachs' retreat. Yes, it's a retreat now. Mom said that there is a magical outdoor labyrinth on the property, nicely hidden within the majestic, and extremely tall pine trees that line the northern part of the property. This forest acts as a shield that guards and protects this mystical and heavenly, golden gateway of healing and enlightenment – as it has come to be known. I'm really excited. I have never been here before today; there always seemed to be a reason why I was never able to come.

As our black, sleek, and very new BMW slows down and is steered to the right side of the road, Mom lets out a long exhale. There stands a limestone-coloured statue of an angel – the Beachs' signpost, and our calling card, at the foot of their driveway's entrance.

"Joshua, Ally, look at that beautiful angel. I feel like we are coming full circle!" Mom cries out, as she puts our wheels in park, and stares at Grams and Gramps in the rear-view mirror.

"Full circle about what?" asks Dad.

"I don't know yet, but I can *feel* it. The answers will come at the right time."

"I hope you're right, Mom. I need some answers. Like, who am I, and what is my purpose in this life? I don't even know what my career path is, and we are being pressured to decide this now, at school." My voice has a bemoaning, *help me* sound to it. That's exactly what I need now: answers. Truthful answers.

"Alice, you are coming-of-age. And, you always were an old soul." Mom replies, in that soothing voice of hers.

"Don't worry, Peach. This will be the weekend where you will begin to find yourself. I promise." Pipes in Dad. I wish he would stop calling me Peach. *Like, I am an adult now.*

"Dad, stop calling me Peach. You know I don't like it."

"Yeah, Joshua. She's not a little girl anymore." That's Mom, always supporting me.

"True. I'm sorry, Ally. But like it or not, you'll always be my little girl."

"*Oh pleeease...*" I'm rolling my eyes now. Dad tends to bring out these kind of reactions in me. I think he enjoys it, the bugger. I can see it now – I'll be fifty years old, and he will be standing there with his cane, calling me Peach. *The old bugger...*

Interesting that Grams and Gramps aren't saying a word. As I turn toward them and look at their well-aged faces, they simultaneously meet my golden-brown orbs with a twinkle in theirs, and they smile. It's like they know something I don't; so what else is new? I feel weird now. Maybe this isn't such a good idea after all.

First Mrs. Beach, then Mr. Beach, slowly walks toward us from the foyer of their house. They begin to greet all of us with gentle bear hugs, and handshakes. And, they start with me.

"This must be Alice! You've grown into such a beautiful young woman. Welcome, welcome." She gives me a big squeeze.

"Thanks, Mrs. Beach."

"Call me Carol, dear. We're on a first name basis here. This is my husband, Sam."

"Hey, Sam."

"Hey, Alice." He extends his hand, and gently shakes mine. I guess he's not an *old hugger.* I mean this with the utmost of respect. Maybe I should become a comedienne...

"This is our daughter, Amy. She is the manager of our humble retreat, thank goodness." Carol explains, as Amy appears suddenly from out of nowhere.

"Hi everyone. Come on in and make yourselves comfortable. There's an organic buffet waiting in the dining room to your right. You may want to settle into your rooms immediately after lunch, as there is a lot planned for some of you, in a short amount of time this weekend." Amy directs us as she speaks, and she seems to have a million thoughts running through her head. "And, I'm going to have to leave you now – duty calls up at the main lodge." Amy is answering her text message while she is saying her goodbyes. Now, she is gone.

"I'm starving. Let's eat." I growl at everyone in a ferocious tongue, like a protective mother bear, leading her cubs to sup. It's strange, I know, but that is how I feel about my family. They are my younglings. I wonder what this means? Hopefully, I will gain some insights, as well as truthful answers, during my nature walk after lunch. *Wow, do I ever sound like Mom...*

It is now two o'clock, on this crystal clear and turquoise blue, brilliantly shimmering and sunny-skied afternoon. I am waiting here at the dock for Amy to arrive, like she promised in her note that she left for me in my room. She said she will direct me into the labyrinth. The labyrinth is also known as The Sanctuary here at the pond, and this floating piece of linked logs – this wooden train track that I am standing on is my first signpost. As I bob-and-weave, I can honestly say that I'm glad I ate a light lunch.

"Hey, Alice." Amy announces her arrival, and I am so startled by her quiet greeting that I almost fall into the water. "Whoa, careful girl!" Thanks Amy, but I don't need a mid-afternoon swim, fully clothed. Maybe some other time.

"Okay, now that you are on solid ground, I am going to direct you into The Sanctuary. But, it's up to you to find your way out, so make sure you follow the gold markers on the trees. When you finish your journey, you will end up right where we're standing. And don't worry, the labyrinth is pretty simple to maneuver – you'll be out in no time." She takes hold of my hand as she speaks, and pulls me onto dry land. Terra Firma.

"Amy, will I find my purpose?"

"Honestly, I don't know. But what I do know is that you'll experience…*magic*."

"Awesome."

"Trust me, it will be. I promise you that."

I feel like I am being lovingly guided by Gaia herself, as I step onto this buffet of humus, and my new life path. *I can feel it.* The watercolours of blended and brushed greens envelop me. I am fanned amongst the ferns as they tickle my pant legs, while I slush through the fallen piles of copper and red leaves at the entrance to The Sanctuary. As I make my way along the muddy path, I see my first marker. It's a gold bow that is attached to the trunk of a curved Oak tree, and it is standing to my right. My way is to the right, and right again.

Okay Spirit, please give me my answers. Who am I? What is my life purpose? What career path should I walk on? I begin to recite The Hail Mary to myself. Maybe now my prayers will be heard, and my questions, truthfully answered. I feel a great sense of *presence* within me now.

Caw, caw caw. As I stop walking and look up, I see a black Raven flying directly towards me. It perches itself on the leaning pine, right in front of me. Okay. Maybe this is a sign. Dang, I wish I brought my copies of *"Animal-Speak" by Ted Andrews*, and *"The Power of Now" by Eckhart Tolle* – my birthday gifts from Mom and Dad. I will have to look up the Raven's meaning when I get back to my room. *Caw, caw caw.* As I make eye contact with the Raven, I am transfixed. I cannot break my stare. Suddenly, I feel a strong urge to close my eyes, and as I do, I feel a deep inner shift. It is as if I just rode down the first drop on a giant roller-coaster. *I'm seeing myself on campus…I'm a professor – just like Gramps was! I am giving a lecture to an ascending hall filled with about three-hundred students, all bright-eyed and sponge-like. They are taking in my teachings, and they continuously stare at me. But what am I teaching?*

Quantum Physics. Hey, imagine that. *Yes, imagine that. Visualize that.* Whoa, these are subtle yet strong thoughts that I am hearing in my mind, and they aren't letting go of me. Maybe this is Spirit talking to me, and I think that it is time for me to start listening.

Okay Spirit, is this my calling? No answer. *Okay, um, Spirit, is this my life purpose?* An electric rush of excitement just ripped up the back of my spine, and my head is tingling. It feels like every hair on my body is standing on end. *The answer is yes.* Experiencing this physical sensation for the first time validates my answer. Hey, maybe this is how I will know the truth, and make better decisions for myself from now on.

I open my saucer-like orbs and look up. There is no sight of the Raven.

This is wild. There is, like, a magical energy here, and I've never experienced anything like this before! As I close my eyes and connect in again, I can't help but ask over and over: *Spirit, who am I?* I'm not getting anything…maybe I am trying too hard. I am just going to let this go for now, and continue walking on my path.

It looks like the sun is in its beginning stages of setting, and I decide that it's time for me to head back to the house. The western sky is beaming down rays of prisms: crystalline amethyst and lapis lazuli-coloured patterns that burst through the trees. These images of gemstones smell like peach cobbler, baking on a sunny and warm afternoon.

…Mom…*ahma, ohma, ahma, ohma, ahma, ohma, ahma, ohma…*

…Gramps…*ahma, ohma, ahma, ohma, ahma, ohma, ahma, ohma…* They are calling me to come back to them now. I should get going.

Crackle-snap…fizz…thwack…snap…fizz-thwack! The flames of this dancing campfire sounds like an orchestra of fireworks, performing an aria on a humid Canada Day celebration at the beach. And yet I can hear the soft lapping tides coming in from the lake. The subtle warmth that emanates from the core of the fire cocoons me, like a furry angora cardigan, giving me an inner sense of safety and comfort.

As I gently rock myself to-and-fro, and listen to my family share their spiritual explorations of the day, I cannot help but wonder – or better yet, be in wonderment of the awesome rebirth and awakening that I experienced only a few hours earlier. Now I am convinced. I can accomplish anything I put my mind, heart, and soul into. With Spirit by my side, there isn't anyone or anything that will stop me. I now promise myself that, from this day forward, I will always try to be kind and true to myself and others. I will act with the highest good in mind; and I will...*love.*

Free Form Poem
I Shall Perform My Miracles

The flood of heartbeat and heaving rushing in,
Tremours of jubilance rock me to-and-fro,
Earth, sky, earth, sky, earth – now Heaven.
Vastness of panoramic turbulence
Silencing the existence that I once was.

Wings are spread like an Eagle, soaring throughout a billowing of
Space and Time,
You have my back –
And I am not alone.

My physicality resonates, like jelly
Vibrating at unfamiliar accelerations.
Strength of body streams into my Spirit –
I am hushed, yet I am traveling at a
Velocity that plummets me forward.

The Transcendence

A jarring reminder of my reality sinks in
As my umbrella deploys, and my
Gentle floating begins.
I now heed the rapture in my roaring –
I begin to feel the awe in my aria,
And the prima in my pirouette of pleasure.

We tip-toe on Terra Firma now,
And I have engaged my heightened rarr.
I shall perform my miracles…
Life begins anew.

Acknowledgments

The spiritual healing and growth concepts and practices, mentioned throughout this book, are gratefully acknowledged. To learn more, please feel free to explore the following authors: James Redfield, Deepak Chopra, Louise L. Hay, Eckhart Tolle, Shakti Gawain, Ted Andrews, and His Holiness the 14th Dalai Lama. For a deeper understanding, you can also participate in any of the following spiritual and holistic healing modalities: meditation, Usui-Do, Network Spinal Analysis, Certified Reflexology, Registered Holistic Nutrition, and Feng shui.

To the reader:

Haiku Medicine 2021

Facing the unknown
With Heart in Hand, faithfully.
Stepping forward now.

And lastly, I would like to express my gratitude and appreciation for all those who have taught and supported me on my journey of spirituality and healing, throughout the years.
We have only just begun.

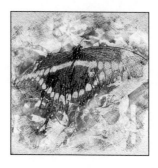

Butterfly 2021 by Mara Recalis

Glossary

On call one and two
A medical resident that is on call day and night.

Slash and burn medicine
Refers to critical care patients, that are operated on.

Works Cited

Glossary: My 2009 interview with an M.D. (Anonymous).

Shakespeare, William. *The Merchant of Venice.* FOLGER Shakespeare Library. Ed.
    Barbara A. Mowat and Paul Werstine. New York, Simon and Schuster, 2010. Print.

ABOUT THE AUTHOR

MARA RECALIS C.R., C.H., R.H.N. is a Canadian poet and writer of fiction. She is a Certified Reflexologist, a Chartered Herbalist, a Registered Holistic Nutritionist, and a Usui-Doka. This is her first novella in *The Transcendence* duology.

CPSIA information can be obtained
at www.ICGtesting.com
Printed in the USA
LVHW071542080822
725434LV00002B/84

9 781039 133808